# PONY PALS

PAT JACOBS

Crabtree Publishing Company

www.crabtreebooks.com

 **Crabtree Publishing Company**
www.crabtreebooks.com
1-800-387-7650

**Published in Canada**
**Crabtree Publishing**
616 Welland Avenue
St. Catharines, ON
L2M 5V6

**Published in the United States**
**Crabtree Publishing**
PMB 59051
350 Fifth Ave, 59th Floor
New York, NY 10118

Published in 2019 by CRABTREE PUBLISHING COMPANY.

First published in 2019 by Wayland
Copyright © Hodder and Stoughton, 2019

**Author:** Pat Jacobs

**Editors:** Victoria Brooke, Petrice Custance

**Project coordinator:** Kathy Middleton

**Cover and interior design:** Dynamo

**Proofreader:** Melissa Boyce

**Prepress technician:** Samara Parent

**Print and production coordinator:** Katherine Berti

**Photographs:**
Alamy: p. 16–17 (top center), 24 (top right)
iStockphoto: p. 19 (top), 21 (bottom right), 25 (top)
Shutterstock: p. 2–3 (center and bottom), 6 (bottom and center right), 8 (top),
11 (bottom right), 12 (top right), 13 (center and bottom left), 16–17 (top), 18 (top
right), 19 (center and bottom), 25 (center), 27 (treats, apple, and horse), 29, 31
All other images courtesy of Getty Images iStock

Every attempt has been made to clear copyright. Should there be any inadvertent
omission, please apply to the publisher for rectification. The website addresses
(URLs) included in this book were valid at the time of going to press. However,
it is possible that contents or addresses may have changed since the publication
of this book. No responsibility for any such changes can be accepted by either
the author or the Publisher.

Printed in the U.S.A./012019/CG20181123

**Dedicated by Katherine Berti**
**To Anna Kantor, Peter MacLeod,**
**and your two stable babies, Charlie**
**the horse and Cosmic, the Little Dude.**

**Library and Archives Canada Cataloguing in Publication**

Jacobs, Pat, author
　　Pony pals / Pat Jacobs.

(Pet pals)
Includes index.
Issued in print and electronic formats.
ISBN 978-0-7787-5729-0 (hardcover).--
ISBN 978-0-7787-5734-4 (softcover).--
ISBN 978-1-4271-2231-5 (HTML)

　　1. Ponies--Juvenile literature.　2. Ponies--Behavior--
Juvenile literature.　I. Title.

SF315.J33 2018　　　j636.1'6　　　C2018-905540-5
　　　　　　　　　　　　　　　　　　　C2018-905541-3

**Library of Congress Cataloging-in-Publication Data**

Names: Jacobs, Pat, author.
Title: Pony pals / Pat Jacobs.
Description: New York, New York : Crabtree Publishing, 2019. |
　Series: Pet pals | Includes index.
Identifiers: LCCN 2018049842 (print) | LCCN 2018050493 (ebook) |
　ISBN 9781427122315 (Electronic) |
　ISBN 9780778757290 (hardcover : alk. paper) |
　ISBN 9780778757344 (paperback : alk. paper)
Subjects: LCSH: Ponies--Juvenile literature. |
　Pets--Juvenile literature.
Classification: LCC SF315 (ebook) | LCC SF315 .J33 2019 (print) |
　DDC 636.1/6--dc23
LC record available at https://lccn.loc.gov/2018049842

# CONTENTS

Your pony from head to tail     **4**

Traditional pony breeds     **6**

Find your perfect pony     **8**

A place to live     **10**

Bedding down and tacking up     **12**

Welcome home!     **14**

Feeding your new friend     **16**

Everyday care     **18**

Pony behavior     **20**

Pony health problems     **22**

Training     **24**

Fun and games     **26**

Pony quiz     **28**

Quiz answers     **30**

Learning more     **31**

Glossary and Index     **32**

# YOUR PONY FROM HEAD TO TAIL

A pony is a small horse. They are tough, intelligent, and not too difficult to take care of. Ponies make wonderful family pets!

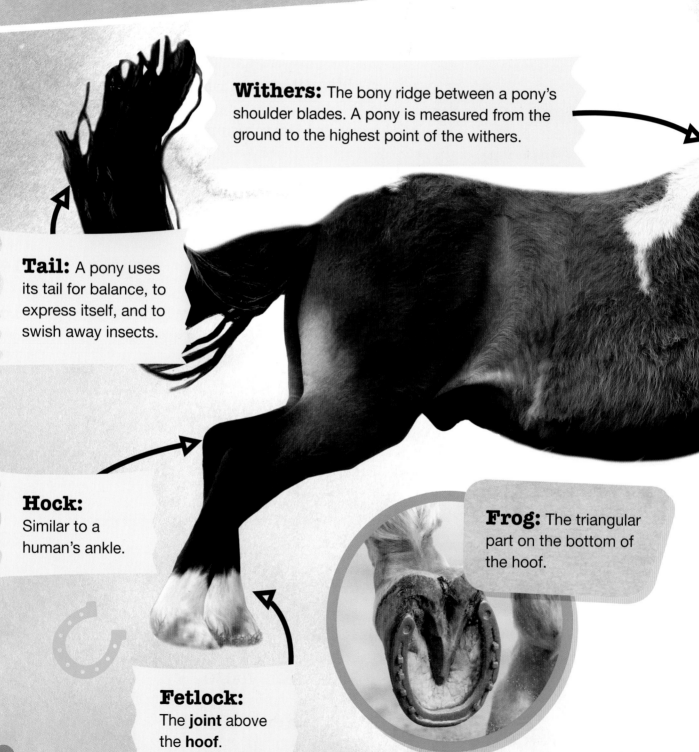

**Withers:** The bony ridge between a pony's shoulder blades. A pony is measured from the ground to the highest point of the withers.

**Tail:** A pony uses its tail for balance, to express itself, and to swish away insects.

**Hock:** Similar to a human's ankle.

**Frog:** The triangular part on the bottom of the hoof.

**Fetlock:** The **joint** above the **hoof**.

**Ears:** Ponies can swivel their ears and pick up sounds all around them. The sensitive area just behind the ears is called the poll.

**Mane:** The thick hair that grows from the top of a pony's neck to its withers. The mane helps to keep the pony warm, drains water away from the pony when it rains, and offers some protection from insects.

**Eyes:** A pony's eyes are on either side of its head. This creates a blind spot directly in front of and behind the pony.

**Muzzle:** This area is very sensitive. It includes the mouth, chin, lips, and nose.

**Cannon:** The part of the leg between the hock and the fetlock.

# PONY FACTS

The unit of measurement for a pony is called a hand. Originally, a hand referred to the width of a person's hand. Today, a hand is 4 inches (10.2 cm) across. A pony stands less than 58 inches (147 cm) tall. That is 14.2 hands, which is read as 14 hands and 2 inches (5 cm).

# TRADITIONAL PONY BREEDS

Ponies typically have sturdy bodies, strong bones, tough hooves, and short legs. They grow a thick winter coat which allows them to live outside year round.

**Dales** ponies are known for their intelligence, strength, and courage. Dales ponies are calm and kind. They have large, tough hooves and strong legs with feathered fetlocks. They are surefooted, meaning they can move easily and safely over uneven ground.

**Dartmoor** ponies are strong, reliable, and **hardy**. They stand up to 12.2 hands high and are usually bay, brown, or black (see color descriptions on page 7). They are gentle and kind, making them excellent ponies for children.

**Pony of the Americas** is a **breed** of pony that grows up to 14 hands high and is known for its spotted coat and gentle personality. These ponies are dependable, calm, patient, and surefooted, making them perfect for any beginning rider.

**Fell** ponies have heavily feathered legs and feet with strong hooves that don't often need shoes. These clever characters make good family ponies, but they can be stubborn. They are surefooted and especially suited to carriage driving.

## COAT COLORS

Ponies' coats come in a variety of colors. Here are a few:

**Bay**—rich-brown body with black legs, mane, and tail

**Chestnut**—reddish-brown with no black points

**Dun**—sandy-colored body with black legs, mane, and tail

**Roan**—an equal mix of white hairs and a pony's basic body color, such as a bay roan

**Gray**—gray ponies have black skin with white or gray hair, and look gray or off-white. Pure white horses have pink skin and are very rare.

**Welsh** ponies have gentle and friendly personalities, making them popular pets for children. They are easy to train and make good carriage-driving ponies. Welsh ponies are intelligent, hardy, and surefooted.

**Connemara** ponies are smart and willing. "Connies" love to jump, but they also do well at everything from carriage driving to **dressage**. These gentle, good-natured ponies are easy to keep, and at up to 14.2 hands, are great for both child and adult riders.

**Hackney** ponies are medium-sized ponies with broad shoulders, smooth backs, and high tails. They are easy to keep, and they have lovable personalities. They are perfect for pulling carriages, but they also make good riding ponies and companions.

**Shetland** ponies stand only up to 10.2 hands high. They can survive harsh conditions, but can also easily become overweight. These little ponies are intelligent and crafty. A bored Shetland will get into all kinds of mischief, so they need to be kept busy!

# FIND YOUR PERFECT PONY

Buying a pony is exciting, but it's easy to fall in love with the wrong one, which can make riding unsafe and less fun. Like humans, ponies are individuals, so take time to find your perfect partner.

## CHOOSE AN EXPERIENCED PONY

A young, inexperienced pony may be cheaper to buy, but it will take time to train and there's no guarantee it will be safe and reliable. It's best to choose one that is at least five years old and has been well trained so you can start riding it straight away. Ponies can be ridden into their twenties, so you will have many years of fun ahead!

## SIZE IS IMPORTANT

When choosing a pony, you should be able to mount it from the ground. When seated, your feet should not be much lower than its belly. Ponies should not carry more than 20 percent of their body weight, including **tack**. It's tempting to buy a larger pony if you're still growing, but it may be difficult to control and it's a long way down if you fall.

# TOP TIPS FOR PONY BUYERS

Ponies are expensive, and the wrong one could be unsafe, so you must choose one carefully. Here are some tips to help you make a great choice:

- Take someone with you who has lots of experience with horses and ponies, and ask their advice.
- Choose a pony to match your skill and fitness level. Your riding instructor may be able to advise on the best breed of pony for you.
- Handle the pony yourself and perform all its day-to-day activities, such as catching, leading, grooming, and tacking up.
- Watch the pony's owner ride it before you try it out. Ask to spend some time alone with your potential new pal.
- Ask about the pony's history. If a pony has changed owners many times, it could point to a health or behavioral problem. Check that its **vaccinations** are up to date.
- If you are seriously interested in buying a pony, ask a vet to examine it. It can be difficult to get **insurance** without a pre-purchase veterinary report.

## BUY OR BORROW

You can borrow a pony from a private owner or a horse charity. The upkeep costs and responsibilities will be the same, but a pony on loan from a charity will be well trained and have had vet checkups. They will be able to offer you support and advice too!

## HEALTH CHECK

- A pony should be curious and alert.
- Its coat should be shiny and smooth.
- The eyes should be clear and bright.
- Its ears should be pricked, held forward or to the side, or flicking backward and forward.
- The nose should be clean and the pony's breathing should be regular and steady.
- The pony should walk comfortably and evenly on all four feet.

# A PLACE TO LIVE

You should have everything ready to welcome your pony to its new home so the move goes as smoothly as possible. If you've never cared for a pony before, it would be a good idea to sign up for a course on horse care.

## STABLING

Ponies are built to live outdoors. They grow thick, waterproof winter coats, and as they **digest** food, their bodies produce heat. Even though ponies love being outside, it's still a good idea to put them in a stable at night or during bad weather. Ponies also need to be inside if they're sick so it's easier to care for them. Stables must be well **ventilated**, and make sure all the door bolts are secure because some clever ponies will learn how to open them!

## PADDOCK PREPARATION

For a proper-sized **paddock**, your pony should have 4,500 square feet (418 square meters) of **grazing** area. Remove things from the paddock that could harm your pony, such as wire, glass, bricks, stones, or poisonous plants. Fill in, or fence off, any holes in the ground. Ponies drink five to 10 gallons (19 to 38 liters) of water a day, so you may need a water tank specially made for horses or ponies.

# BOARDING

If you don't have room for a pony at home, you can keep it at a boarding stable, which is a rented stable space. Boarding a pony will mean it has some horsey companions, and you can also get help and advice from the staff and other pony owners. There are different levels of boarding depending on how much you are willing to pay and how much of your pony's care you want to do yourself.

## BOARDING CHECK

- Self-care boarding includes grazing and use of a shelter or stable. The owner is responsible for all the pony's care.

- Part or assisted boarding includes some help from staff, such as feeding, **turning out**, and **mucking out**.

- Full boarding is expensive. It normally includes bedding and feed, and stable staff are responsible for all of the pony's care, including exercise.

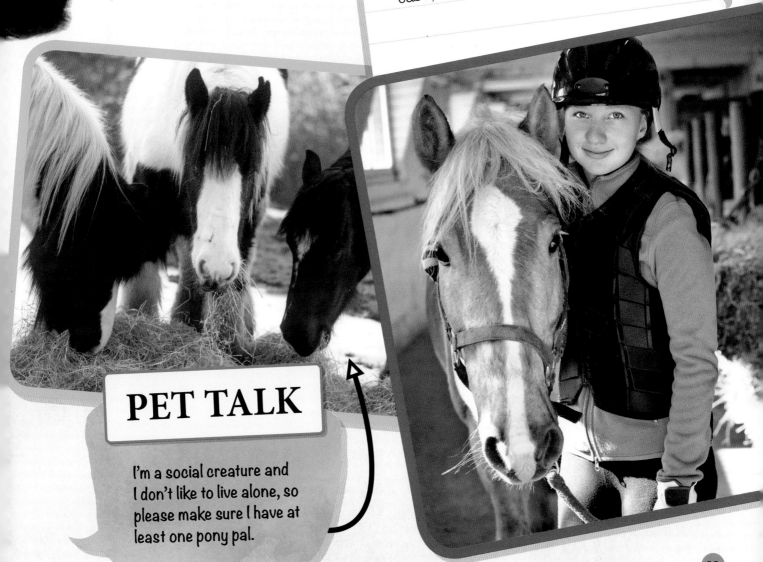

## PET TALK

I'm a social creature and I don't like to live alone, so please make sure I have at least one pony pal.

# BEDDING DOWN AND TACKING UP

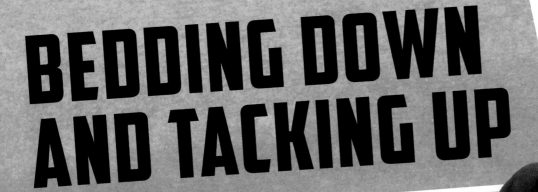

Get some bedding to make your pony pal a soft, warm bed when it arrives. This is also the time to get all the equipment you'll need to ride and care for your new friend.

## A COMFORTABLE BED

Ponies can sleep standing up, but they do like to lie down sometimes, so they need a soft bed to protect their joints. Choosing the best bedding for your stable will depend on your storage space and whether your pony is sensitive to dust or has allergies.

**Straw** is cheap but messy to store, and it takes up a lot of space. Some ponies are allergic to it, while others like to eat it. It makes good garden **compost**.

**Wood shavings** are easy to store and ponies won't eat them. Droppings and wet shavings should be removed quickly to avoid a buildup of **ammonia**. Shavings take longer to rot down than straw, and cheap brands contain a lot of dust.

**Shredded paper** is useful for ponies that have allergies, but a large amount is needed to make a good bed. It gets blown around easily, which can make the area around the stable untidy.

**Wood pellets** are **eco-friendly**, dust-free, and very absorbent. Wet patches are easy to spot and quick to remove, and pellets compost quickly. The pellets need soaking in water before use, which takes extra time.

**Rubber matting** is dust-free and easy to clean with a hose. It's expensive, but there are no extra costs. Extra bedding may be needed in a drafty stable. The stable needs good drainage and, without bedding, your pony may get dirty.

# ESSENTIAL EQUIPMENT

You can save money by buying some equipment secondhand, but make sure everything is thoroughly cleaned before use. Secondhand saddles should be checked by a saddler to make sure they fit properly. Some sellers include a pony's saddle and tack.

## EQUIPMENT CHECK

- A well-fitting saddle
- A bridle and bit
- A grooming kit
- Feed and water buckets
- Mucking-out equipment
- A first aid kit: including bandages, cotton pads, and antiseptic
- Insect repellent

Saddle

Bridle

Bit

Reins

Stirrup

# RIDING WEAR

A well-fitting riding hat will protect you from serious injury. Make sure yours meets the current safety standards—it's best to buy from a shop with a professional fitter. Your boots should have smooth soles and a small heel so your foot doesn't slip through the stirrups. They must be sturdy enough to protect your foot if your pony steps on it. It is also a good idea to wear gloves to protect your hands and to get a good grip on the reins.

# WELCOME HOME!

Moving to a new home can be very stressful for a pony. It has to get used to new companions, a different stable, and a new paddock. Try to find out as much as you can about your new friend's routine so you can introduce any changes slowly.

## A NEW DIET

At first, feed your pony the same food it's used to eating. If possible, take some hay from its old home and gradually add your own to reduce the risk of colic (see page 23). If you're turning your pony out, restrict it to just a few hours, then increase it slowly. Make sure your pony drinks enough. It may need to get used to the taste of your water, so try adding a little sugar or molasses.

## QUARANTINING A NEW ARRIVAL

If you have other horses or ponies, let them see the new pony from a distance at first. It's important to quarantine your new pony for at least two weeks to avoid spreading diseases or infections. Use different food and water buckets, as well as grooming and mucking-out equipment. If you're caring for several horses or ponies, change your clothes and clean your boots when you move between them for the first few weeks.

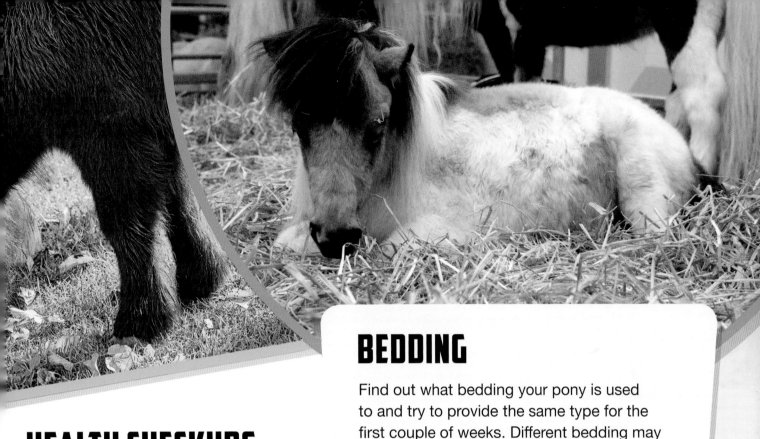

## HEALTH CHECKUPS

Register your new pony with a vet and a **farrier** as soon as possible in case a problem arises. Try to avoid the stress of dental treatments, vaccinations, and **shoeing** while it gets used to its new home. It's normal for a pony's behavior to change after moving, but if it shows signs of a cough, high temperature, or loss of appetite, call your vet immediately. Once your pony has settled in, get it checked for worms.

## BEDDING

Find out what bedding your pony is used to and try to provide the same type for the first couple of weeks. Different bedding may affect a pony's breathing system, leading to a cough and runny nose. Some people recommend bringing a little of your pony's old bedding to its new home, so it smells familiar.

## PET TALK

Grooming is a good way to make friends with me.

# FEEDING YOUR NEW FRIEND

Ponies need to eat small amounts frequently, so it's better to give them four small meals than two large ones. They can be greedy creatures, and eating too much rich food may cause serious health problems.

## WEIGHT WATCHING

A pony's natural food is grass. In the wild, ponies put on weight during the summer when grass is plentiful, and lose it over the winter when there is less grass. The food we give ponies today is much richer than the rough grass they would naturally eat, and because they are often in a stable and kept warm during the winter, they don't burn off the extra fat. If your pony is overweight, give it less food in the winter and more time outdoors so it burns energy to stay warm.

## THE BEST DIET

Ponies have small stomachs and long digestive systems that break down tough plants. They need bulky food such as grass to keep their food moving through their intestines or the food can get stuck, causing colic. While grass and hay should be the main part of the diet, if a pony is exercised regularly it will need small amounts of special feeds, such as cereal or sugar beet. A pony's digestive system is full of friendly **bacteria** that break down plant foods, so always change its feed gradually to give its system a chance to adapt.

## HOW TO FEED

Scattering food on the ground allows a pony to eat in a natural way, but it's wasteful and soil may be picked up with the feed, so it's best to put feeds in a bucket. Hay can be left in a pile on the ground—although there will be some waste, this is safer than using a hay net because ponies can get their feet or necks caught in the net.

## POISONOUS PLANTS

Some common plants can be very dangerous for ponies. Learn to recognize them and remove them, or fence them off. They include ragwort, rhododendron, foxglove, yew, privet, laurel, bracken, buttercup (harmless in hay), lily of the valley, deadly nightshade, laburnum, St. John's wort, sycamore, and oak (leaves and acorns).

## PET TALK

I love treats such as carrots and apples, but please cut them lengthwise and take the cores out of apples, or they may get stuck in my throat.

# EVERYDAY CARE

Caring for a pony is hard work, and you'll probably spend more time mucking out and grooming than riding. Are you up for the challenge?

## PONY CARE ☑

**Daily tasks:**
- Mucking out
- Grooming
- Exercising
- Feeding
- Topping up water troughs
- Picking out hooves
- Checking for signs of illness or injury

**Weekly tasks:**
- Removing droppings from pasture
- Checking paddocks for hazards
- Scrubbing out food and water containers

## PONY CARE CALENDAR

Here's a list of jobs that are essential to keep your pony fit and healthy—and they have to be done whatever the weather! Your pony will also need regular visits from the farrier and vet for hoof trimming, re-shoeing, worming, dental care, and vaccinations.

## MUCKING OUT

Stables need cleaning at least once a day. You'll need a hayfork, rubber gloves, a shovel, a broom, and a wheelbarrow for this job. Move any droppings and dirty bedding into the barrow, sweep the floor, and let it air out for as long as possible. Then add the clean bedding and top it up. If you can't turn the pony out, move it to one side of the stable and clean half of it at a time. Keep your tools away from your pony's feet!

# FOOT CARE

You should check your pony's feet every day and remove any dirt or stones using a hoof pick (see right). Always work toward the toe so you don't harm your pony if the pick slips. Ponies that are worked on roads or hard ground may need shoes to protect their hooves. Hooves should be trimmed by a farrier every six weeks for **shod** ponies and every ten weeks for unshod ponies.

# GROOMING

Grooming keeps your pony's coat and skin clean and healthy. It also strengthens the bond between the both of you, and it's a chance to check for injuries. Use a **curry comb** in small circular movements in the opposite direction to the hair growth to loosen dirt. Flick away the dirt and loose hair with a **dandy brush**, then use a soft body brush to remove anything left on the surface of the coat. Clean your pony's face with a sponge or cloth, and use a separate sponge or cloth for the tail area. Never share brushes and cloths between ponies because this can spread infections. Finally, untangle the tail and mane with your fingers, then brush or comb them.

## PET TALK

Sometimes when you're grooming me you might touch a very sensitive area and I may kick, so please stand at my side, and never behind my back legs.

19

# PONY BEHAVIOR

Ponies communicate with one another using body language. By giving signals to other members of the **herd**, they are able to establish their position within the group without fighting.

## YOU ARE THE BOSS

Wild ponies live in herds ruled by a leader who decides the position of all the other group members. Pet ponies also need a leader and, as ponies are large, strong animals, it's important that the leader is their owner.

## PUSHY PONIES

Ponies that are challenging your authority will crowd and push you, walk in front when you're leading them, and nip, bite, kick, or step on your foot. The best way to show a pony that you're the boss is by earning its respect, which means you should be kind but firm. Ponies can sense fear, hesitation, and anger, so always act calmly and confidently, and if a pony tries to move into your space, push it back.

## PET TALK

If you come straight toward me, looking me in the eye, I will probably run in the opposite direction because this means "go away" in pony language.

# EXPRESSIVE EARS

Ponies have very sensitive hearing and their ears are a clue to what they are thinking:

- Ears pricked and facing forward mean a pony is happy and interested in something.
- Ears lowered to the sides normally mean a pony is relaxed.
- Flicking ears show that a pony is listening and paying attention.
- Ears pinned flat against the neck are a warning sign that the pony is annoyed or unhappy and you should beware.

# TAKING FLIGHT

Ponies are always on the lookout for **predators** and are ready to flee if something frightens them. They have sharp senses of smell and hearing, so if they suddenly react they may have heard a noise you didn't. Pricked ears, wide eyes, flared nostrils, and a raised head are a warning that a pony may bolt. If you're a nervous rider, your pony may sense this and be more jumpy. You can take lessons to gain confidence.

# PONY HEALTH PROBLEMS

Ponies don't make a fuss when they're in pain, so you need to be aware of any changes in your pal that might mean it's unwell. Get to know your pony's normal heart rate, temperature, and breathing rate so you can spot if something is wrong.

## LAMINITIS

Laminitis is a painful condition that affects ponies' hooves. It starts with slight **lameness** and can get so bad that the bone of the foot sinks through the sole and the pony has to be put to sleep. It can be caused by a past injury, stress, infection, or being worked for too long on a hard surface. Being overweight or a diet with too much sugar can also cause it. To avoid this, be sure not to overfeed your pony, and restrict grazing on sweet new spring grass. Treatment should be given as soon as possible, so contact your vet immediately if your pony shows signs of lameness.

# COLIC

Colic means stomach pain, and it's common among ponies. Wild ponies graze on low-energy food throughout the day. Pet ponies often have just two feeds of rich food a day, and their guts haven't adapted to the change. Other causes can be dental problems, worms, stress, or a change of diet. Signs of colic include rolling, lying down for long periods, looking at or kicking the stomach, curling the upper lip, sweating, and restlessness. Call the vet if you think your pony may have colic.

# STRANGLES

Strangles is a common infection of the nose and throat that is easily spread. A pony with strangles will have a high temperature, loss of appetite, yellow pus draining from the nose, and **abscesses** may appear on the sides of the throat and head. Ponies can recover after a few weeks with good nursing.

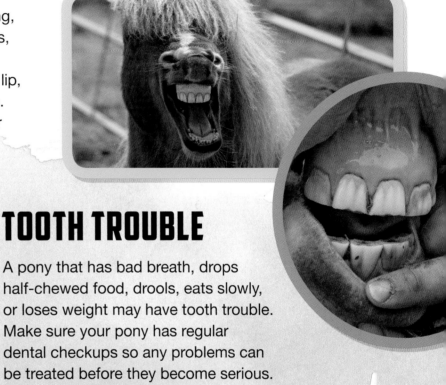

# TOOTH TROUBLE

A pony that has bad breath, drops half-chewed food, drools, eats slowly, or loses weight may have tooth trouble. Make sure your pony has regular dental checkups so any problems can be treated before they become serious.

Pony manure infected with roundworms.

Feed your pony pureed apple from a large syringe as a treat from time to time so it won't be scared of syringes when it needs worming treatment.

# WORMING

Ponies can swallow worm eggs while they graze, which develop into worms in the gut. Worms lay millions of eggs that end up in the pony's droppings, ready to be swallowed by another pony. Ponies get large and small redworms, roundworms, pinworms, threadworms, tapeworms, lungworms, and bots. Worms are becoming resistant to medicines, so have droppings tested to check the number of eggs before giving medication. Removing droppings from paddocks regularly helps reduce the eggs your pony eats.

# TRAINING

Your pony needs to learn good ground manners before you start riding it. This may take time and patience, but riding a pony that doesn't respect you is very dangerous.

Halter

## GROUND MANNERS

A pony with good ground manners will stay out of your personal space, stand patiently, and allow you to clean its feet and groom it. It will also accept having a harness called a halter put on its head to be led around, and stand still as you put on a bridle and saddle for riding. If a pony bites, kicks, or rears, it's not safe to ride.

## EARN THEIR TRUST

Wild ponies trust their leaders and follow whatever they do, so to gain your pony's respect you need to show that you're a confident leader. Ask for help from an experienced horse or pony keeper. Once your pony recognizes you're the boss, don't let it get away with bad behavior. But never train a pony by losing your temper or hurting it. Not only is it cruel, but ponies are strong and they may fight back.

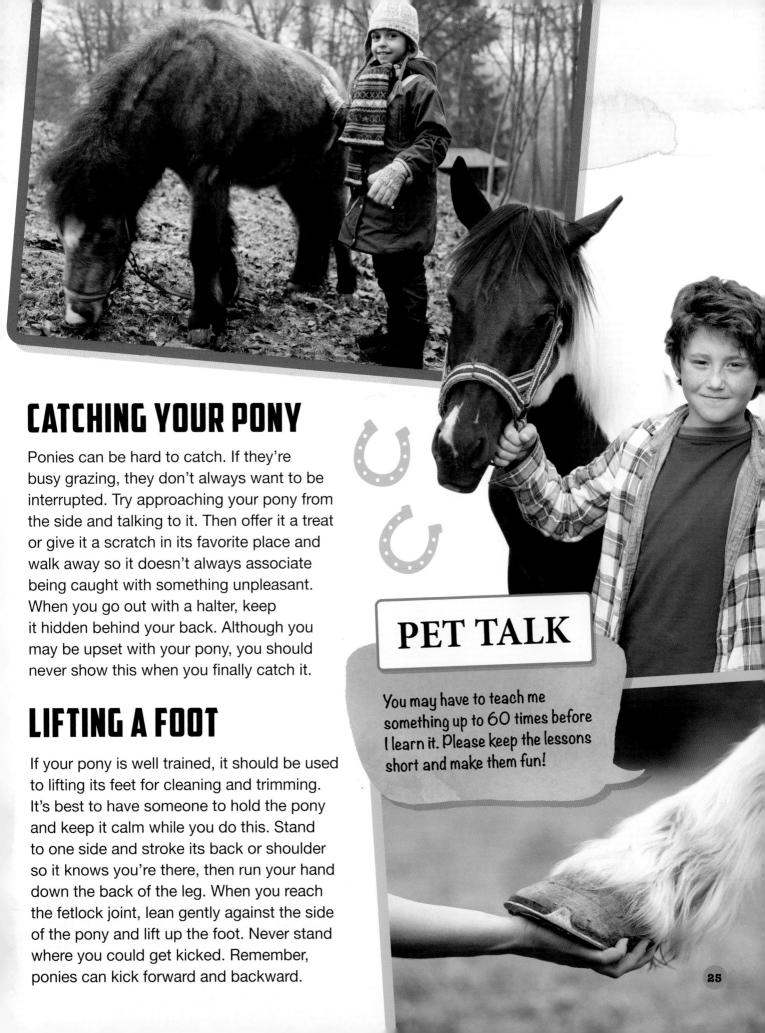

# CATCHING YOUR PONY

Ponies can be hard to catch. If they're busy grazing, they don't always want to be interrupted. Try approaching your pony from the side and talking to it. Then offer it a treat or give it a scratch in its favorite place and walk away so it doesn't always associate being caught with something unpleasant. When you go out with a halter, keep it hidden behind your back. Although you may be upset with your pony, you should never show this when you finally catch it.

# LIFTING A FOOT

If your pony is well trained, it should be used to lifting its feet for cleaning and trimming. It's best to have someone to hold the pony and keep it calm while you do this. Stand to one side and stroke its back or shoulder so it knows you're there, then run your hand down the back of the leg. When you reach the fetlock joint, lean gently against the side of the pony and lift up the foot. Never stand where you could get kicked. Remember, ponies can kick forward and backward.

## PET TALK

You may have to teach me something up to 60 times before I learn it. Please keep the lessons short and make them fun!

25

# FUN AND GAMES

One of the main reasons for getting a pony is to work as a team and have fun together! Taking part in games is good for bonding and it stops your pony from getting bored.

## PONYTASTIC GAMES

Here are some games you can play alone with your pony, or you can get together with friends to compete against each other. Set up your arena first and make sure you have room to turn safely.

**Pole-bending race**—Set up five poles (or cones) in a straight line, about 23 feet (7 meters) apart. The pony and rider should weave through the poles to the end of the line, then turn around and come back. The fastest time wins, but there's a five-second penalty for touching a pole.

**Potato race**—Place a barrel for each rider at the far end of the course. Put two potatoes on each barrel. The riders gallop to pick up one potato at a time, then place it in their bucket back at the starting line. The winner is the first rider to get both potatoes in their bucket.

# MAKE A PONY TOY

Rinse out a large plastic milk container and cut some holes in the side that are just a little larger than your pony's treats. Put some treats into the container and screw the lid back on. Your pony will have lots of fun playing with the container and trying to get the treats to fall out.

# MAKE YOUR OWN PONY TREATS

These homemade treats are packed with all your pony's favorite foods. You can experiment with your own ingredients, but never give your pony chocolate, maple syrup, rhubarb, or milk.

**Ingredients:**
1 grated apple (seeds removed)
2 grated carrots
1/4 cup (60 ml) molasses
2 tbsp (30 ml) vegetable oil
1 cup (240 ml) whole-wheat flour
1 cup (240 ml) rolled oats
1 tsp (5 ml) salt

Preheat the oven to 350°F (180°C).

Mix the apple, carrots, molasses, and oil together in a large bowl, then add the flour, oats, and salt. Mix together and roll into small balls. Line a baking sheet with waxed paper and bake the treats for about 20 minutes until they are golden brown.

**Egg and spoon race**—Riders balance an egg on a spoon and hold it out to the side while someone instructs the riders to perform different moves. The last rider with the egg still on their spoon wins.

## PET TALK

I need to be kept busy, otherwise I'll make my own fun—and you may not like that!

# PONY QUIZ

By now you should know lots of things about ponies. Test your knowledge by answering these questions:

**1** **What are a pony's withers?**

a. The area around the tail
b. The bony ridge between a pony's shoulder blades
c. The joint above the hoof

**2** **Where would you find a pony's frog?**

a. On its foot
b. On its back
c. On its head

**3** **What is the maximum size for a pony?**

a. 12.6 hands
b. 15 hands
c. 14.2 hands

**4** **What is special about a Shetland pony?**

a. It is very small
b. It has pink skin
c. It is not very intelligent

**5** **Which plant is poisonous for ponies?**

a. Ragwort
b. Foxglove
c. Both of these

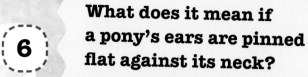

**6** What does it mean if a pony's ears are pinned flat against its neck?

a. It is annoyed
b. It is relaxed
c. It is happy

**10** What may be wrong if your pony rolls around kicking its stomach?

a. It may have worms
b. It may have strangles
c. It may have colic

**7** Which body part is affected if a pony gets laminitis?

a. Tail
b. Hooves
c. Stomach

**8** How often should you check your pony's feet?

a. Once a week
b. When it starts limping
c. Every day

**9** Where should you stand to groom your pony or clean its feet?

a. At its side
b. Behind it
c. In front of it

29

# QUIZ ANSWERS

**1** What are a pony's withers?

**b.** The bony ridge between a pony's shoulder blades

**2** Where would you find a pony's frog?

**a.** On its foot

**3** What is the maximum size for a pony?

**c.** 14.2 hands

**4** What is special about a Shetland pony?

**a.** It is very small

**5** Which plant is poisonous for ponies?

**c.** Both of these

**6** What does it mean if a pony's ears are pinned flat against its neck?

**a.** It is annoyed

**7** Which body part is affected if a pony gets laminitis?

**b.** Hooves

**8** How often should you check your pony's feet?

**c.** Every day

**9** Where should you stand to groom your pony or clean its feet?

**a.** At its side

**10** What may be wrong if your pony rolls around kicking its stomach?

**c.** It may have colic

# LEARNING MORE

## BOOKS

MacAulay, Kelley and Bobbie Kalman. *Ponies.*
Crabtree Publishing, 2005.

Marsh, Laura. *National Geographic Readers: Ponies.*
National Geographic Children's Books, 2011.

Ransford, Sandy. *Horse and Pony Factfile*. Kingfisher, 2006.

## WEBSITES

**www.ponymag.com**
This site for *Pony Magazine*
offers tons of information,
videos, and games all
about ponies!

**www.thesprucepets.com/
horse-and-pony-care-
by-the-day-1886011**
Visit this site for tips and
information on how to
take the very best care
of your pony pal.

# GLOSSARY

**abscess** A painful swelling on the skin, filled with pus, usually caused by an infection

**ammonia** A strong-smelling gas that is produced when urine reacts with bacteria

**bacteria** Microscopic living things that are found everywhere

**breed** A group of living things with common ancestors

**compost** To use decayed matter as fertilizer for plants

**curry comb** A comb with short teeth used to bring dirt to the surface of a pony's coat

**dandy brush** A hard-bristled brush used on ponies with very thick coats

**digest** The process of food being broken down and absorbed in the body

**dressage** Training a pony to perform a series of movements

**eco-friendly** Not harmful to the environment

**farrier** Someone who trims and shoes ponies' hooves

**grazing** When animals roam about and eat what is found, such as grass

**hardy** Able to withstand hardship

**herd** A group of animals that travel together

**hoof** The thick, horn-like covering on a pony's foot

**insurance** An agreement paid by a person to a company that promises to pay money to the person if their property is lost or damaged

**joint** A point where two bones fit together to allow motion

**lameness** Limping or having trouble walking normally

**mucking out** Removing dirty bedding from a stable

**paddock** An enclosed area where animals can roam

**predator** An animal that hunts other animals

**shod** Equipped with shoes

**shoeing** The act of placing shoes, usually made of metal, on a pony's feet

**tack** Equipment used to ride or lead a pony, such as saddles and bridles

**turning out** Putting a pony outside to graze

**vaccination** An injection to provide protection from disease

**ventilated** Allowing fresh air into a room

# INDEX

bedding 11, 12–13, 15, 18
coat 4, 6, 7, 9, 10, 19
colic 14, 16, 23
Connemara 7
Dales 6
Dartmoor 6
dental 15, 18, 23
disease/infections 14, 19, 22, 23
ears 5, 9, 21
eyes 5, 9, 20, 21
Fell 6
fetlock 4, 5, 6, 25
food 10, 14, 16–17, 18, 23, 27

frog 4, 19
games 26–27
grazing 7, 10, 11, 14, 22, 23, 25
grooming 9, 13, 14, 15, 18, 19, 24
Hackney 7
hay 14, 16, 17
health 9, 15, 16, 18, 19, 22–23
hooves 4, 6, 7, 10, 19, 22
insurance 9
kick 19, 20, 23, 24, 25
laminitis 22
leading 8, 13, 20, 24

legs 4, 6, 7, 13, 19
livery 11
mount 8
mucking out 11, 13, 14, 18
muzzle 5
nose 5, 9, 15, 23
paddock 10, 14, 18, 23
poisonous plants 10, 17
Pony of the Americas 6
quarantine 14
riding 7, 8, 9, 10, 11, 13, 18, 24

saddles 13, 24
Shetland 7
stable 10, 12, 13, 14, 16, 18
strangles 23
straw 12, 13
tack 8, 9, 13
tail 4, 7, 19
training 8, 9, 24–25
vaccinations 9, 15, 18
vet 9, 15, 17, 18, 22, 23
water 10, 12, 13, 14, 18
Welsh 7
withers 4
worming 15, 18, 23